A SOUL NOT ECLIPSED

An ANTHOLOGY of ORIGINAL POEMS

LISHA SIMMONDS

A SOUL NOT ECLIPSED
AN ANTHOLOGY OF ORIGINAL POEMS

iUniverse books may be ordered through booksellers or by contacting:

iUniverse
1663 Liberty Drive
Bloomington, IN 47403
www.iuniverse.com
844-349-9409

ISBN: 978-1-6632-0226-0 (sc)
ISBN: 978-1-6632-0228-4 (hc)
ISBN: 978-1-6632-0227-7 (e)

Library of Congress Control Number: 2020918034

Print information available on the last page.

iUniverse rev. date: 10/19/2020

Crescent Moon

A sliver of a yellow moon,
A scintilla left of light—
I'm mesmerized by the cosmos,
The power of star movement across the sky at night.

Who is he?

He
Is the patient one,
The kind one,
The strong one,
The empowering one,
Doesn't-flinch-under-the-gun one,
Relishes-me-even-when-I'm-not-fun one,
Believes-in-me-every-minute-shade-or-sun one.
He is the doesn't-run one.
He is the search-is-done one.
He is the best one.

He is my already-won one.

Effect and affect

A spontaneous smile erupts on my face.
Images of you pixelate, focus in place.
I am as enamored now as ever in our paradigm,
Trusting in commitment we nurtured over time,
Respect, and mutual kindness.
We share a careful mindfulness.
We are well matched, my love,
To one another,
Deliberate and protective of.

Homemade homebody

You and you alone
Have been
And always will be
Where I am home.

Lung of my life

I want my last breath
To be like the breath
I take after a moment of pure exhilaration,
Like a spectacular sunset,
Where my eyes are in disbelief of such splendor.
Or a ravishingly delicious kiss,
Where the only occupation of my mind
Is the taste of you on my lips.
Yes, that breath
After that moment where I am
Collecting myself and my senses,
Relishing afterglow before meeting my maker to say
Thank you for a spectacular life.

Mistaken matrix

Refusing to chase that clock
Down another rabbit hole,
But
He kept calling me Alice.
"Isn't Alice a boy's name?"
I said.
I adopted a white rabbit
To teach me how to hop to it,
But it died
When it fell in a hole
Near the pool.
I gave up
Searching catacombs
For signs of life
And
Walked away.

Full moon's surf reCreation

Extraordinary.
The roar speaks volumes
Up,
Down to specific rays,
Laser into the water's surface,
Like diamonds dancing under the spotlight for a gemologist.
I can't help but sing,
"How great thou art,
How great thou art."

Personal rePercussions

These noticeable echoes
That reverb
Are iconic to me now,
Neither
Disturbing nor flattering.
The echo is simply what is.

Construction zone

You have my love,
Which means
I will be your scaffold.
When your heart is in a state of restoration,
There is no quid pro quo.

Eyes that endlessly adore

A study of dog,
Resplendent with loyalty.
We do what we do to love them,
So we are who they believe us to be.

Pain On Pointe

Her arch so turned so concave,
Her turn out
Hip perfect.
Her toes, bloody and misshapen,
Still point.
The discipline,
Labor of love,
To be as light as air
On a pinhead.

Fiddle me this

My imagination
Plays a violin
Of joy.

Misplaced benefit of the doubt

"What's new?"
You.
You are new.
"And do you love me now?"
I'm in love, yes, but
You don't know him.
"I don't?"
No.
You buried him.
"I did?"
Yes.
And my heart was buried with who you used to be.
"I never was."
Yes, I know.
I created you.
I saw through you.
I gave you the benefit of the doubt.
Then I woke up.

Visual field

Less to say
Each and every day,
More to be,
More to see,
With eyes of a different hue,
Filtering with less of me and more of you.

See? reflected, self image

Acceptance creates
A mirror
On a lake:
Clarity,
Serenity.
The restlessness
Yields to rest,
A willingness to be like water.

Link me up

Hold my hand.
Don't let go.
I went too high
Without
A parachute
And now I know why.

Grief Suffocation

My heart is still beating.
I feel that rhythm in my head.
But I think my rib cage
Got smaller;
Either that, or after you left,
A boa constrictor took up residence,
Wrapping itself around my lungs.

Soul on soul

My light met your light,
And suddenly I believed
In reincarnation,
Because I felt like I had known you
In a former body.
Mostly I knew my heart
Would be safe,
Nourished by your soul.

Surf the sync

Sync with me, baby.
I'd rather decline diluted wine
Or lukewarm kisses.
I've decided to wait for the embrace of my wishes,
The one that can be gentle when I'm falling to pieces,
The one that like a barometer knows how we complete us.
The heat rises.
We ride that fire and darkness that hide us.

Softness renovates

Stay soft
Because
Rubber balls bounce
On impact,
And
Crystal shatters
If it falls off a shelf.

Solar storms

The cataclysmic events will come and go,
Best endured in your arms,
Because your arms are home.
And home is always the best place to be
When storms crush spirits.
Our bond will always be stronger forged in fire.

Present in that moment by moment

I ran faster.
I jumped higher,
Climbed farther.
Tired,
I stopped.
I heard the most wonderful sound:
Silence.
I wept for the happy
I wanted,
And
Nothing else entered my mind.

Unfulfilled needs yield

I climbed and climbed and climbed,
And then
I didn't want to climb anymore.
I wanted to crawl
Under quilts with you
With a fireplace
And a Labrador
And not much else except coffee in the morning.

Misperceptions: feminine as fatale

Women who are strong
Are not attached to brooms
Despite generalizing to the contrary.
We do not all dispatch flying monkeys to
Proxy despair
Or witch-striped socks
To wear
With stilettos instead of ruby slippers.
Femme emphatic happens all the time
Without a cold mouthpiece of resentment.
Takes practice.
Just watch.
Women will come out of the walls like a boss.

Before the crash

When we were young,
My heart felt warm beside your heart,
My cheek, which rested on your sternum,
As protected by your rib cage
As much as by your own vital organs.
I thought I meant enough
To be that valued
To you,
By you.

Potential parent plumage

Birds of paradise
Spread their wings
Without flying
To dance ritually a dance,
Attempting
To impress a mate for pairing.
Their conjugal tango is risky.
What if she chooses another?
She may be coy
But only
To be certain
His coupling dance isn't just flirtin'.

Parachute

There you are, floating,
Dropping
Through the sky
Into me.
I am still motionless,
I am afraid of impact.
I trust
Your rate of speed
Slows
To soften the moment when your body
Finds mine.
We flow,
A physical tangle
Indistinguishable from you
As we joyously
Drop,
Locked with God's love
We find forever.

Tribal find

Is a muse a moment?
A memory?
A mind?
Or rather a mindful experience?
To demonstrate to us,
We seek
Others who share
The same need for our depths.

Bypassing a Dangling participle

All these moments
Where time wrecked me,
I've decided to just let it be.
People come,
And
People go.
I never thought you'd be though
Part of past-tense perfect.

Indifferent

The apathy
Made me smile.
Your illusory presence was gone.
The ghost of you left no impression on
Me.
Karma had no power.
I wasn't crying anymore.

Intimacy

This need to touch,
This requirement to be touched,
This affection—
This is real.

All pure
Is as is.
I feel
For you revealed.

Ocean below

The light shifted.
Once a blue crest
Is now green,
Still flipping around
Like popcorn exploding from heated steam.
Waves,
Handshake, and move on to shore;
More like a dance than a chore.
Seabirds choose their path too
To fly by gust,
Not as much by sight—
A faster speed above wing.
Much like a surface of a wave
As the shallow reaches below and slows.
Water is physically a phenomenon of energy flow,
A gorgeous shape of change.

Shield to healed

Gatekeeper,
Angel of freedom and intensity,
Harbinger of light,
Sentinel of the lawful,
Healer of the afflicted.

Mind up

Darkness steals only from the vaults of light.

Walk the talk

Say,
"I love you."
Prove it's true.
Repeat,
Especially when the one you love has a day of blue.

Curious dove

She lay down, did the dove,
Atop and above,
Turned head
To watch me.
Solo,
She understood all I needn't say,
Her contentedness apropos
Of the sunshine that illuminated her face.
She did a little yoga stretch,
Each leg and each wing,
As she righted herself.
She left
Then,
But I knew I had met her in that moment.
She chose to watch me
Diligently.

Performance

I saw the ocean today.
She had no audience.
The beach was eerily desolate.
She danced anyway.

Oceanic

From a protected position,
I observed the ocean.
She waved.
She waves.
I smile.
Joy is just being mesmerized by her wardrobe changes,
Her wardrobe mistress being the weather.

Totality of interdependent circumstances

Aggregate moments
Of your infinite patience
Shielded me while I regrouped,
Promulgating my belief in me,
Launching my confidence in me.
You're my blessing.
You're my future tense,
My best efforts,
My desire to do better,
My dangling participle,
My split infinitive.
My success, you love.
My wild, you love.
My strength, you love.
My fragility, you love.
My insistence, you love,
As I so impatiently desire to forever love you
With all my heart.

Mentaphysical kind of love

There you go again,
Occupying space in my temporal lobes
Multiple times an hour,
Where I nestle you most lovingly in my mind,
Because for the first time
In my life,
Thinking about you—a man—
Makes logical sense in my head.
At the same time,
My face flushes crimson.
Butterflies flutter near my ribs.
My heart beats faster,
And
My skin is wide awake with anticipation,
Because you are just so appealing to every sensory
Receptor in the inventory of my body.

Goofy footed

I suppose by admission of how I feel for you,
Evidenced by my walking into walls
At the sight of you like a distracted teenager.
I may set myself up for humiliation
Of biblically Moses proportions,
But this time,
This time,
I care little about what anyone thinks.
You're worth the slipping on a banana peel,
A moment I've dreaded since middle school.
You're that one guy,
That one-in-ten-billion guy,
Who is the lightening bolt to my thunder.

Solving a mystery, the mastery of you

What makes you smile?
It's okay. I'll enjoy figuring it out,
Though it may take a while.
What's your favorite color?
It's okay. I'll find the paint that makes your day.
What's your best memory?
It's okay.
Rest assured that same memory
Will become my recipe, our way
To taste sweet forever.
What's your family's favorite legacy?
It's okay.
After feeling comfortable with me,
Your mom will enjoy sharing every replay.
You'll be a happy boy,
Because I'm going to be your highway to joy.

Your shielded wings

You gave me the love and safety
I used for the courage
To recognize
The exchange
Of protected and brittle,
For unaffected warmth and openheartedness
Are more me
Than I ever believed I could possibly be.
Receptively
For this,
I thank you.

Sacred self

With surgical precision
You lovingly transformed my life.
Return
To a sacred place
Where I always best belonged.
Clearer vision,
A truer-to-myself existence:
Living fully,
Living loved.

Consistently you

Some men stick the landing.
They're the committed ones,
The ones with whom love grows,
The ones who love your life in whole,
The ones who know how strong you are,
How to love you when you're weak.
Or when you push them away because you're too proud
To remember "He's on my team,"
The ones who will always sit on your side of a table,
The ones whose hearts need to be protected.

Alternating strength pillars

What makes you strong
Makes me strong.
I promise you this though.
If you ever feel weak,
I will be strong,
Because that's how we roll.

Life is like sandpaper

Holding the truth burned my hand.
The seesaw burned my soul.
But the end result is my true self
Is worthy,
Purple, and
Scarred.

Friday.

Yay.

Let's be joyous, okay?

I see the "we" of you and me. We have our oath to each other's best interests. We have a love of hiking. Mountains. Breathing. Sharing a pod hammock until neither of us is young enough to get out without help.

I see us slow, slow dancing. I see gentle. I see our family and friends happy to see us happy.

I see me bringing you coffee in the morning exactly as you like it. When you realize I'm in the shower alone, you join me.

We have animals that have babies like sheep and horses.

We have a garden.

We have dogs and chickens and cats and an owl, which took up residence in the barn and scares the baby cow.

We created a slope of lawn, and we have a tractor mower I love to ride around, and we have an attachment to make mulch out of the clippings because it's sustainable.

We have solar panels and use candles.

We have a wine collection, but neither of us really follows the labels very closely. We like what we like.

We travel to New Zealand and fall in love with the culture.

We travel to Italy and choose not to go out because it's so much more romantic in bed.

We invite your mom along on outings to raves, where we have to cook our own food.

We bring our sons along to ride horses with us on the trails in the foothills. And we are happy. And at peace. And harmonious. And the tears stay away unless they're tears from laughter.

This is the "we" I see. My love.

Joy.

I like being goofy to draw laughter from people I love. I like being a registered independent voter because black or blue or red isn't appealing. I like puppies, even when they pee on the floor. I like children because they haven't yet learned to be cynical. I like religious services because everybody is facing in the same direction and sings and prays as one. I like trees just because I like them.

I like gardens that burst out of their designated cubbyholes and grow in messy, informal ways like they're defying an order to be in a militarily precise row as planted.

I like—no, I love—people who forgive me, especially when I just get caught in the roulette wheel that scrambles my brain, and vertigo is like kryptonite.

I love men who don't deliberately make me cry.

I love people who appreciate little gestures of love. I love people who, no matter what, stick by me.

I adore people who have compassion and understand that which goes right by me does not hurt me.

I love the people who are waiting. I pray every day they know I love them and that nothing I've done did I do intentionally to hurt them.

Eternally grateful. Lisha.

CPSIA information can be obtained
at www.ICGtesting.com
Printed in the USA
BVHW071353091120
592841BV00004B/751

9 781663 202260